Blastoff! Readers are carefully developed by literacy experts to build reading stamina and move students toward fluency by combining standards-based content with developmentally appropriate text.

 Level 1 provides the most support through repetition of high-frequency words, light text, predictable sentence patterns, and strong visual support.

 Level 2 offers early readers a bit more challenge through varied sentences, increased text load, and text-supportive special features.

 Level 3 advances early-fluent readers toward fluency through increased text load, less reliance on photos, advancing concepts, longer sentences, and more complex special features.

★ **Blastoff! Universe**

Reading Level

 Grade K

 Grades 1–3

 Grade 4

This edition first published in 2022 by Bellwether Media, Inc.

No part of this publication may be reproduced in whole or in part without written permission of the publisher. For information regarding permission, write to Bellwether Media, Inc., Attention: Permissions Department, 6012 Blue Circle Drive, Minnetonka, MN 55343.

Library of Congress Cataloging-in-Publication Data

Names: Green, Sara, 1964- author.
Title: Rivers / Sara Green.
Description: Minneapolis, MN : Bellwether Media, 2022. | Series: Blastoff! readers. Our planet Earth | Includes bibliographical references and index. | Audience: Ages 5-8 | Audience: Grades 2-3 | Summary: "Simple text and full-color photography introduce beginning readers to rivers. Developed by literacy experts for students in kindergarten through third grade"-- Provided by publisher.
Identifiers: LCCN 2021011411 (print) | LCCN 2021011412 (ebook) | ISBN 9781644875254 (library binding) | ISBN 9781648344930 (paperback) | ISBN 9781648344336 (ebook)
Subjects: LCSH: Rivers--Juvenile literature.
Classification: LCC GB1203.8 .G743 2022 (print) | LCC GB1203.8 (ebook) | DDC 551.48/3--dc23
LC record available at https://lccn.loc.gov/2021011411
LC ebook record available at https://lccn.loc.gov/2021011412

Text copyright © 2022 by Bellwether Media, Inc. BLASTOFF! READERS and associated logos are trademarks and/or registered trademarks of Bellwether Media, Inc.

Editor: Rebecca Sabelko   Designer: Jeffrey Kollock

Printed in the United States of America, North Mankato, MN.

Table of Contents

What Are Rivers? 4
Plants and Animals 12
People and Rivers 16
Glossary 22
To Learn More 23
Index 24

What Are Rivers?

Rivers are streams of **freshwater**. They are found around the world.

Rivers move from high to low places. They flow in **channels**. Rivers can be straight, or they can curve.

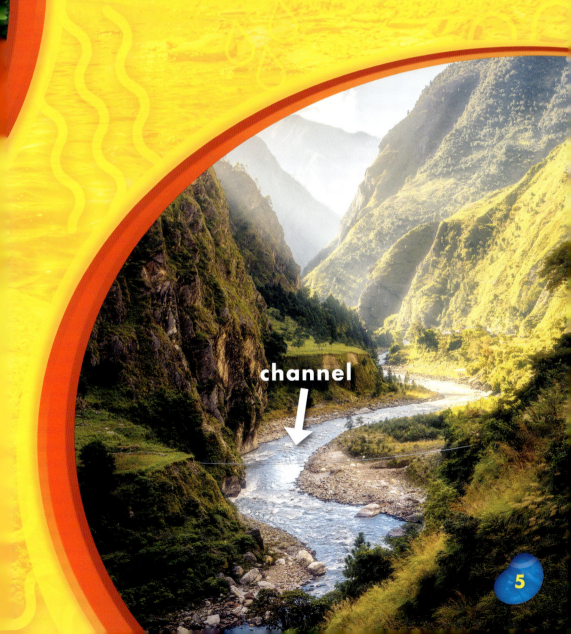

channel

river source

River **sources** are often **springs**, lakes, or melting ice. Water trickles downhill as streams. Streams join to form rivers.

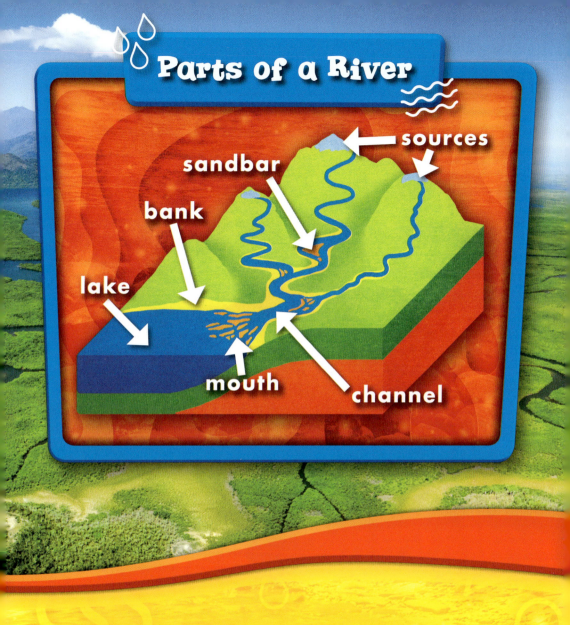

River **mouths** meet lakes, oceans, or other rivers. They may also spread into **wetlands**.

Rivers have **currents**. Currents are strongest when they flow over steep land. Rivers with a lot of water have powerful currents, too.

Narrow channels often have stronger currents. **Obstacles** may slow currents down.

Nile River

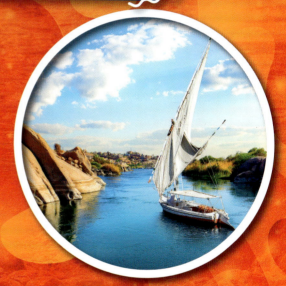

Famous For
- Longest river in the world

Sources
- Kagera River, Lake Tana, and Lake Victoria

Length
- About 4,132 miles (6,650 kilometers)

Africa

Rivers change over time. River **bends** form where **banks** wear down. Currents carry rocks and sand that collect to form **sandbars**.

Missouri River

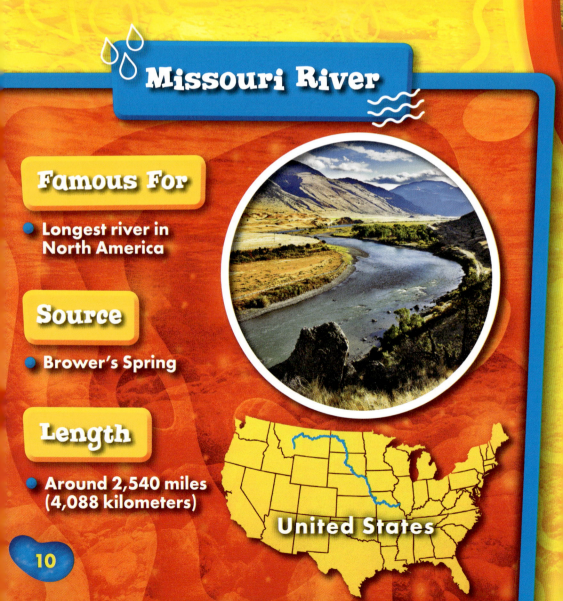

Famous For
- Longest river in North America

Source
- Brower's Spring

Length
- Around 2,540 miles (4,088 kilometers)

United States

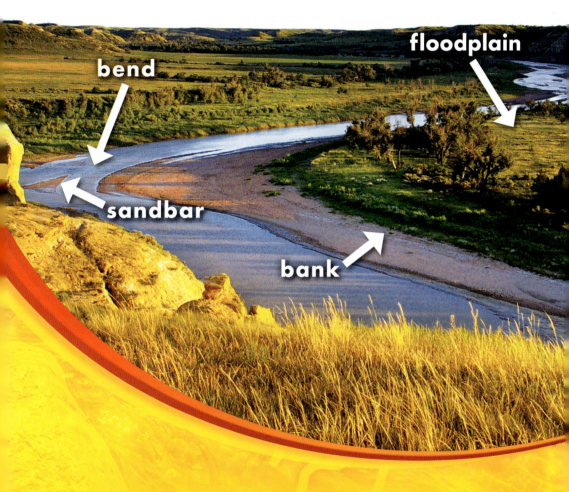

Rivers can flow over their banks to create **floodplains**. Rushing river waters can carve deep valleys.

Plants and Animals

sockeye salmon

Rivers are important to animals and plants. Fish nibble on food that floats on the water. Birds dive to grab fish.

Hippos soak in cool water to escape heat. Beavers build homes in rivers.

River Animals

- hippopotamus
- North American beaver
- Amazon river dolphin
- bald eagle

Trees, reeds, and grasses grow along river banks. They provide homes for nesting birds and other small animals.

mallard ducks in nest

Roots hold soil in place, and they help keep rivers clean.

People and Rivers

People around the world use rivers. Rivers provide water for drinking, cooking, and bathing. Farmers use rivers to water crops. **Dams** help create **electricity**.

People also use rivers for fishing, kayaking, and other sports.

Rivers face many threats. People dump waste into the water. Overuse and **climate change** can cause rivers to dry up.

People and animals suffer when rivers are harmed. Water becomes unsafe for drinking. Animals' homes are destroyed.

How People Affect Rivers

- Waste makes water unsafe for drinking

- Overuse and waste destroy animals' homes

- Overuse and climate change dry up rivers

People can protect rivers. They can collect trash. They can also keep unsafe liquids out of drains.

Rivers are important to plants, animals, and people. It is important to keep them safe!

Glossary

banks—land on the edges of rivers

bends—curves in rivers

channels—paths rivers take

climate change—a human-caused change in Earth's weather due to warming temperatures

currents—water moving in rivers

dams—structures built by people that block a river's flow

electricity—a form of power that travels through wires and is used to operate machines and lights

floodplains—low, flat lands along rivers that flood when rivers overflow

freshwater—water that is not salty

mouths—places where rivers end

obstacles—things that block a pathway

sandbars—areas of sand formed in water by currents

sources—places where rivers start

springs—places where water naturally flows from the ground

wetlands—lands that are covered by shallow water, such as a marsh or swamp

To Learn More

AT THE LIBRARY

Anthony, William. *River Food Webs.* New York, N.Y.: Greenhaven Publishing, 2021.

Murray, Julie. *Animals in Streams & Rivers.* Minneapolis, Minn.: ABDO Publishing Company, 2020.

Pettiford, Rebecca. *Floods.* Minneapolis, Minn.: Bellwether Media, 2020.

ON THE WEB

FACTSURFER

Factsurfer.com gives you a safe, fun way to find more information.

1. Go to www.factsurfer.com.

2. Enter "rivers" into the search box and click 🔍.

3. Select your book cover to see a list of related content.

Index

animals, 12, 13, 14, 19, 21
banks, 10, 11, 14
bends, 10, 11
channels, 5, 9
climate change, 18
currents, 8, 9, 10
dams, 16, 17
effects, 18, 19
farmers, 16
floodplains, 11
formation, 6, 10
ice, 6
lakes, 6, 7
location, 4
Missouri River, 10
mouths, 7
Nile River, 9
obstacles, 8, 9
oceans, 7
overuse, 18
people, 16, 18, 19, 20, 21
plants, 12, 14, 15, 21
protect, 20, 21
sandbars, 10, 11
shape, 5, 10
sources, 6
sports, 16
springs, 6
streams, 4, 6
uses, 16
valleys, 11
waste, 18, 20
water, 4, 6, 8, 11, 12, 13, 16, 18, 19
wetlands, 7

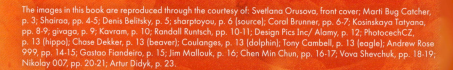

The images in this book are reproduced through the courtesy of: Svetlana Orusova, front cover; Marti Bug Catcher, p. 3; Shairaa, pp. 4-5; Denis Belitsky, p. 5; sharptoyou, p. 6 (source); Coral Brunner, pp. 6-7; Kosinskaya Tatyana, pp. 8-9; givaga, p. 9; Kavram, p. 10; Randall Runtsch, pp. 10-11; Design Pics Inc/ Alamy, p. 12; PhotocechCZ, p. 13 (hippo); Chase Dekker, p. 13 (beaver); Coulanges, p. 13 (dolphin); Tony Cambell, p. 13 (eagle); Andrew Rose 999, pp. 14-15; Gastao Fiandeiro, p. 15; Jim Mallouk, p. 16; Chen Min Chun, pp. 16-17; Vova Shevchuk, pp. 18-19; Nikolay 007, pp. 20-21; Artur Didyk, p. 23.